HISTORY ON THE HIGH SEAS

ABOARD THE AMISTAD

BY CAITIE MCANENEY

Gareth Stevens PUBLISHING

Please visit our website, www.garethstevens.com. For a free color catalog of all our high-quality books, call toll free 1-800-542-2595 or fax 1-877-542-2596.

Library of Congress Cataloging-in-Publication Data

Names: McAneney, Caitie, author.
Title: History on the high seas : aboard the Amistad / Caitie McAneney.
Description: New York : Gareth Stevens Publishing, 2020. | Includes index.
Identifiers: LCCN 2018051339| ISBN 9781538237908 (pbk.) | ISBN 9781538237922 (library bound) | ISBN 9781538237915 (6 pack)
Subjects: LCSH: Amistad (Schooner)–Juvenile literature. | Slave trade–America–Juvenile literature. | Slave trade–Sierra Leone–Juvenile literature. | Slave insurrections–United States–Juvenile literature. | Fugitive slaves–Legal status, laws, etc.–United States–Juvenile literature.
Classification: LCC E447 .M38 2020 | DDC 326.097309034–dc23
LC record available at https://lccn.loc.gov/2018051339

First Edition

Published in 2020 by
Gareth Stevens Publishing
111 East 14th Street, Suite 349
New York, NY 10003

Designer: Katelyn E. Reynolds
Editor: Therese M. Shea

Photo credits: Cover, pp. 1, 5 New Haven Colony Historical Society and Adams National Historic Site/Ibn Battuta/Wikipedia.org; cover, pp. 1–24 (porthole and wood background) Andrey_Kuzmin/Shutterstock.com; cover, pp. 1–24 (wood sign) ESB Professional/Shutterstock.com; cover, pp. 1–24 (brass plate) photocell/Shutterstock.com; pp. 2–24 (old paper) Kostenko Maxim/Shutterstock.com; pp. 4–24 (old notebook) BrAt82/Shutterstock.com; p. 7 Universal History Archive/UIG via Getty Images; p. 9 10topvector/Shutterstock.com; p. 11 STR/AFP/Getty Images; p. 13 Interim Archives/Getty Images; p. 15 MPI/Getty Images; p. 17 (main) Hulton Archive/Getty Images; p. 17 (inset) Rainer Lesniewski/Shutterstock.com; p. 19 courtesy of the Library of Congress; p. 21 HO87875/Wikipedia.org.

Printed in the United States of America

CPSIA compliance information: Batch #CS19GS: For further information contact Gareth Stevens, New York, New York at 1-800-542-2595.

CONTENTS

WORDS IN THE GLOSSARY APPEAR IN **BOLD** TYPE THE FIRST TIME THEY ARE USED IN THE TEXT.

HAUNTING HISTORY

The *Amistad* is a ship with a haunting history. Its story tells of the horrors of the slave trade and of a group of slaves who successfully **rebelled** against their fate. Ripped from their homes in Africa, they took a stand on the *Amistad*.

By the time the *Amistad* began its final journey in 1839, slavery had been in the Americas for over 200 years. About 12.5 million Africans had been seized from their homelands and sent to the Americas as part of the slave trade.

CREWMAN'S LOG

In this log, or record, you'll read a bit about the history of the ship and the people who were on board during the rebellion. These writings, from a sailor's viewpoint, are based on facts.

THE *AMISTAD* WAS A SCHOONER ABOUT 120 FEET (37 M) LONG. A SCHOONER IS A SAILING SHIP WITH AT LEAST TWO MASTS, WHICH ARE THE POLES THAT SUPPORT THE SAILS.

STOLEN

The story of the *Amistad* rebellion begins in West Africa. In early 1839, dozens of people in what was then the British colony of Sierra Leone were forced to march to a slave depot, or holding area, called Lomboko. Some had been captured in war. Some were made slaves as punishments for crimes. Still others were kidnapped, or taken illegally, from their homes.

An African leader rounded up these men and women for a Spanish slave trader named Pedro Blanco. About 500 of these future slaves were forced onto a ship called *Tecora*.

CREWMAN'S LOG

The slaves we brought onto the ship are treated worse than animals. After weeks at that slave depot, they seem like ghosts before they even walk onto our ship.

SLAVES WERE SOMETIMES KEPT FOR WEEKS AT SLAVE DEPOTS. THEY WERE CHAINED, STARVED, AND BEATEN BEFORE THE VOYAGE, OR JOURNEY, EVEN BEGAN.

CRUEL CONDITIONS

The *Tecora* was a slave ship. Like most slave ships, the **captives** were packed tightly together below deck and shackled, or chained, with little food and water and no fresh air. **Disease** spread quickly. Over 1 million Africans died on journeys like this. The dead were dumped in the ocean.

The *Tecora* was bound for Cuba, a Spanish territory in the Caribbean. Slavery was legal there, but **importing** slaves was not. The slave traders had a plan. They would pretend their African captives were native Cuban slaves.

CREWMAN'S LOG

More than 500 Africans are packed body to body. They're chained around their ankles, wrists, and neck with metal shackles. They can't even stand.

TRANSATLANTIC SLAVE TRADE

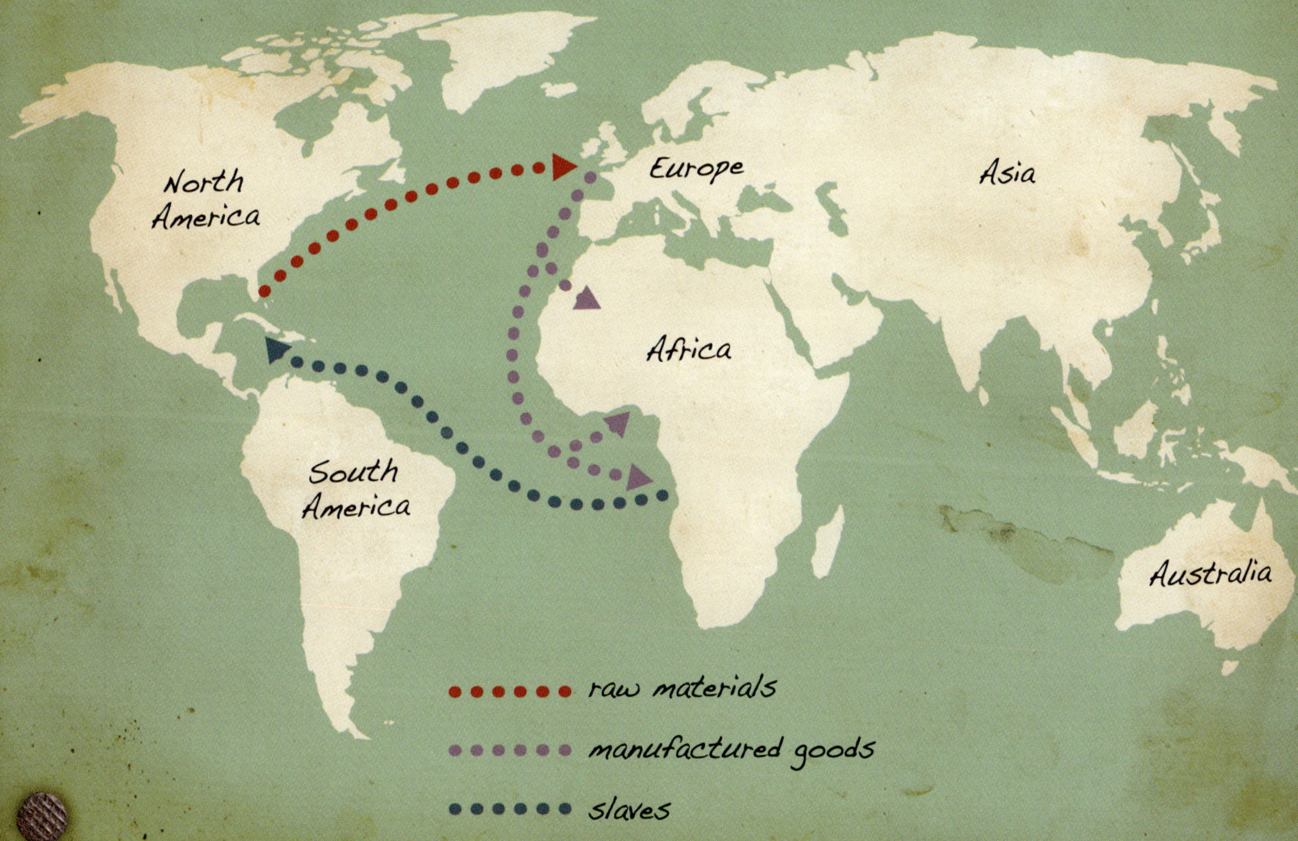

THE TRANSATLANTIC SLAVE TRADE WAS A SYSTEM OF TRADE BETWEEN AFRICA, THE AMERICAS, AND EUROPE. AS THIS MAP SHOWS, EUROPEAN GOODS WERE TRADED FOR AFRICAN SLAVES, WHO WERE TAKEN TO THE AMERICAS. THE AMERICAS SUPPLIED EUROPE WITH RAW MATERIALS, SUCH AS SUGAR AND COTTON.

ONTO THE AMISTAD

It took 2 months for the *Tecora* to reach Havana, Cuba. There, two Spanish men—José Ruiz and Pedro Montes—bought 53 of the slaves, including women and children. On June 28, 1839, these Africans were loaded onto the *Amistad*, which was bound for Puerto Príncipe, Cuba.

The captives were treated with **cruelty** on this voyage, too. They later reported that the cook told them they'd be chopped up and eaten. Crewmembers poured salt and gunpowder into the slaves' wounds. The slaves were pushed to their limits.

CREWMAN'S LOG

Ruiz and Montes knew they bought those slaves illegally. The British sail the coast looking for such unlawful slave trade. We had to leave Havana at night and sneak up the coast of Cuba to avoid them.

THIS IS A REPLICA, OR MODEL, OF THE *AMISTAD*. REPLICAS SHOW PEOPLE WHAT SOMETHING WAS LIKE LONG AGO.

A NIGHT OF REVOLT

The 53 African slaves aboard the *Amistad* were helpless at first. They were shackled on the ship for several days. Then, on July 2, 1839, a 25-year-old African named Sengbe Pieh, also called Joseph Cinqué, used a nail he found to get out of his shackles. He helped the other slaves escape their chains as well.

The slaves killed the cook first and then the captain and most of the crew. It happened so fast that the crew didn't even have time to get their **weapons**.

CREWMAN'S LOG

The uprising was the scariest moment of my life! The captain killed a slave, but was then killed himself. When the slaves found me, I put my hands up to let them know I didn't want to fight.

SENGBE PIEH BANDED TOGETHER AFRICANS FROM NINE DIFFERENT **ETHNIC GROUPS** TO FIGHT FOR THEIR FREEDOM ON THE *AMISTAD*.

TAKING OVER

The captives had complete control of the *Amistad*. They let José Ruiz and Pedro Montes live. Unable to find their way by themselves, the slaves ordered the Spaniards to sail them all the way back to Sierra Leone.

Unfortunately, the plan didn't work. Ruiz and Montes lied to them. They didn't sail for Africa. Instead, they headed north to the United States, hoping to be saved. The *Amistad* sailed for 63 days with little water or food on board. Some Africans died.

CREWMAN'S LOG

Spending months on the water isn't easy. But without enough food and water, it's become downright deadly. Ruiz and Montes tricked the slaves. They sailed east during the day and northwest at night.

WHAT HAPPENED ON THE *AMISTAD* WAS RECORDED IN NEWSPAPERS LIKE THIS ONE.

WAITING IN JAIL

A US Navy ship found the *Amistad* near Long Island and took it to New London in Connecticut, a state where slavery was still legal. Then, the slaves were taken to the city of New Haven, Connecticut.

The slaves found themselves in another hard place—jail. They were forced to wait there until a court decided their fate. After reading about the Africans in newspapers, curious people paid to see them. **Abolitionists** worked to free the slaves. However, others, including US president Martin Van Buren, wanted them returned to Cuba.

LEWIS TAPPAN WAS ONE OF THE ABOLITIONISTS WHO HELPED THE SLAVES, INCLUDING FINDING THEM **LAWYERS** AND TEACHING THEM ENGLISH.

THE TRIALS

Questions arose about the slaves: Should they be returned to their "owners"? Should they be tried for murder? Should they go free since they were taken to Cuba illegally? A **federal** court in Hartford, Connecticut, ruled that the Africans were unlawfully kidnapped and had the right to fight for their freedom.

Some powerful people disagreed with the court and wanted a different decision. Finally, the case went to the US **Supreme Court**. The decision, again, was that the Africans should be freed. Abolitionists helped the surviving 35 Africans return to Sierra Leone.

CREWMAN'S LOG

I attended the slaves' trial at the Supreme Court. John Quincy Adams argued for 7 hours over 2 days. His speeches were very powerful!

AT THE SUPREME COURT TRIAL, FORMER PRESIDENT JOHN QUINCY ADAMS ARGUED FOR THE SLAVES' FREEDOM.

REMEMBER THE AMISTAD

What happened on the *Amistad* shows the cruelty of the slave trade. Slaves were seen as property and were sometimes treated even more poorly than livestock. However, the court cases that followed the *Amistad*'s final voyage were a sign of shifting views in the United States.

At the end of the American Civil War in 1865, slavery was officially ended in the United States. Blacks would continue to fight for rights and equal treatment, however. Today, the *Amistad* remains a **symbol** of their long struggle for freedom.

CREWMAN'S LOG

The Amistad was sold after the trial and renamed Ion. No one knows what happened to it after that. There were many slave ships over the years, but the Amistad is one that I will always remember.

THIS MONUMENT TO THE *AMISTAD* STANDS IN NEW HAVEN, CONNECTICUT.

GLOSSARY

abolitionist: one who fights to end slavery

captive: one who is captured and kept as prisoner

cruelty: actions that cause pain or suffering to others on purpose

disease: illness

ethnic group: a community made up of people who share a common race, country, religion, language, or cultural background

federal: having to do with the national government

importing: bringing goods into a country to be sold

lawyer: someone whose job it is to help people with their questions and problems with the law

rebel: to fight to overthrow a higher authority

Supreme Court: the highest court in the United States

symbol: a picture, shape, or object that stands for something else

weapon: something used to fight an enemy

FOR MORE INFORMATION

Books

Hopper, Whitney. *Slavery in the United States: The "Abominable Trade."* New York, NY: PowerKids Press, 2016.

Worth, Richard. *The Amistad Revolt and the Transatlantic Slave Trade.* New York, NY: Enslow Publishing, 2016.

Websites

The Amistad Court Case
www.ct.gov/kids/cwp/view.asp?a=2573&q=392830
Learn more about the *Amistad* court case on this Connecticut website.

Amistad: How It Began
www.nps.gov/articles/amistad-how-it-began.htm
Read an account of the *Amistad*'s last journey.

Discovering Amistad
kpcnotebook.scholastic.com/post/discovering-amistad
Follow a kid reporter as she visits a replica of the *Amistad*.

INDEX